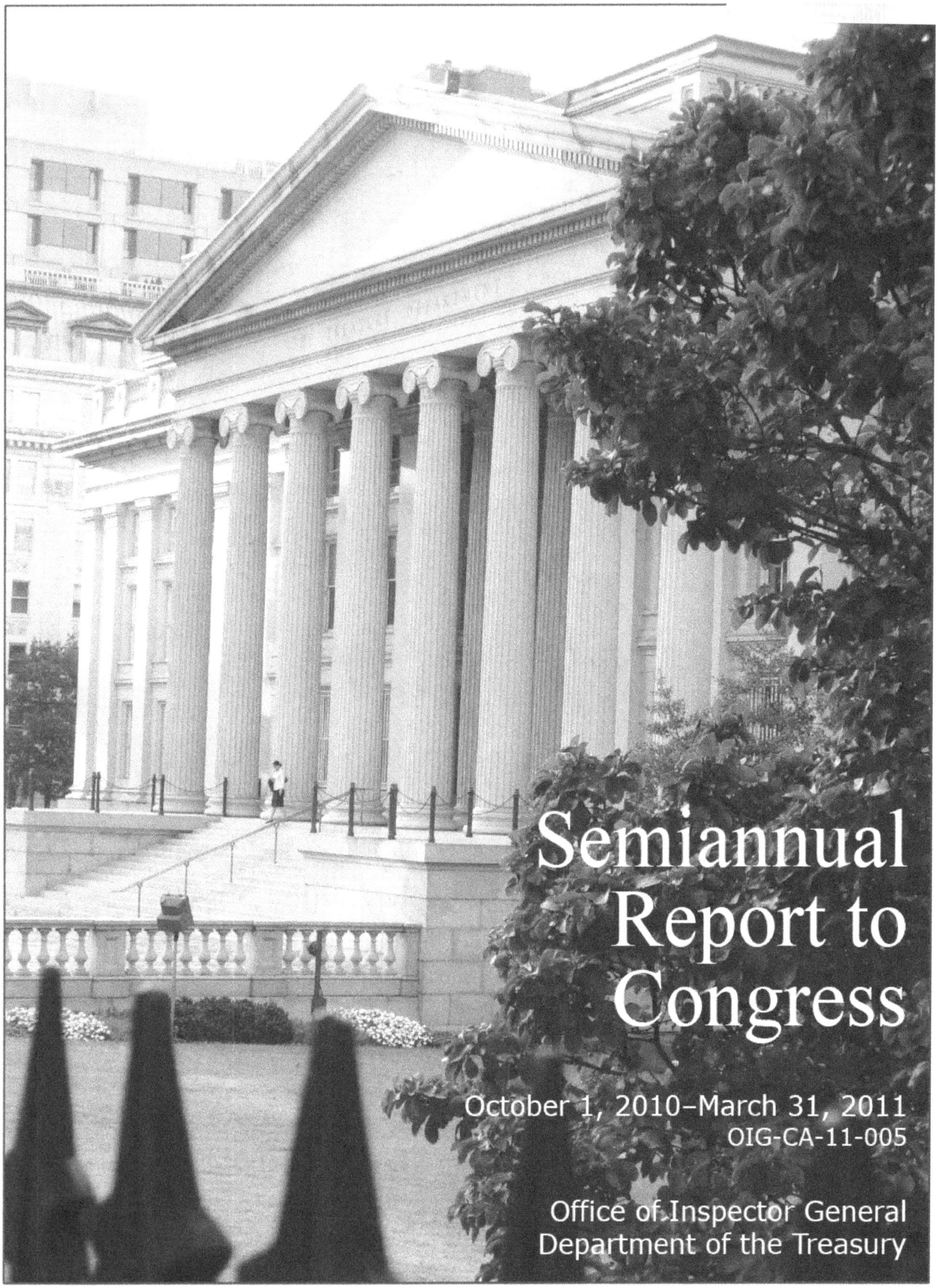

Semiannual Report to Congress

October 1, 2010–March 31, 2011
OIG-CA-11-005

Office of Inspector General
Department of the Treasury

Highlights

During this semiannual reporting period, the Office of Audit issued 65 products, and recommended that $19.6 million in funds be put to better use. The work by the Office of Investigations resulted in 9 arrests and 8 convictions. Some of our significant results for the period are described below.

- We completed a review with the Offices of Inspector General (OIG) of the Federal Deposit Insurance Corporation (FDIC) and the Board of Governors of the Federal Reserve System (FRB) of the Joint Implementation Plan for the transfer of Office of Thrift Supervision (OTS) functions to the Office of the Comptroller of the Currency (OCC) and other federal banking regulators. That plan, prepared by OCC, OTS, FDIC, and FRB, and our review, were required by the Dodd-Frank Wall Street Reform and Consumer Protection Act. We concluded that the plan generally conforms to the provisions of the act, but noted that the plan did not address the prohibition against involuntary separation or relocation of transferred OTS employees for 30 months. We also reported that certain details of the plan need to be worked out to ensure that OTS employees are not unfairly disadvantaged and an orderly transfer of OTS's powers, authority, and employees can be effectively accomplished.

- KPMG LLP, under our oversight, issued an unqualified opinion on the Department of the Treasury's fiscal year 2010 financial statements. The auditor reported 4 significant deficiencies. One significant deficiency related to financial systems and reporting at the Internal Revenue Service is considered a material weakness. The other 3 significant deficiencies are related to the Department's financial management practices, the Office of Financial Stability's financial accounting and reporting, and the Financial Management Service's information system controls.

- In January 2011, we and the FRB OIG jointly responded to a congressional request for information on Treasury's activities related to the standing up of the Consumer Financial Protection Bureau (CFPB) and the Secretary of the Treasury's authorities under the Dodd-Frank Act with respect to CFPB until a Director is confirmed by the Senate. CFPB was established by the Dodd-Frank Act as an independent bureau within FRB.

- We were informed that an individual was creating and passing fraudulent checks totaling approximately $1 million through the Treasury Direct Program while utilizing a Treasury bank routing number on each fraudulent check. As a result of an OIG investigation, the individual was indicted in federal court in October 2010 on 16 counts of wire, bank, and mail fraud violations. The individual pled guilty to 1 count of bank fraud; sentencing is pending.

- In another scheme involving Treasury Direct, OIG special agents executed an arrest warrant to an individual attempting to flee the country from the Dulles International Airport. The individual was later indicted. Additionally, the U.S. Attorney's Office issued seizure warrants for five fraudulent Treasury Direct accounts which resulted in the recovery of over $781,000.

This semiannual report includes a section "Bank Failures and Nonmaterial Loss Reviews" to fulfill our reporting requirement in section 987 of the Dodd-Frank Act related to reviews by our office of failed Treasury-regulated financial institutions with losses to the Deposit Insurance Fund that are under $200 million. We performed 11 nonmaterial reviews during this reporting period.

Message From the Inspector General

In our Semiannual report for September 30, 2010, I highlighted some of the new programs and responsibilities that both Treasury and my office have been given as the Administration and the Congress continue to address the Nation's efforts to recover from the financial crisis and deep recession. Over the past 6 months my office has been busy addressing those new responsibilities, as well as continuing to meet our mandate to conduct failed bank reviews.

As required by the Dodd-Frank Act, we have established the Council of Inspectors General for Financial Oversight (CIGFO), which I chair. CIGFO is now fully functioning and recently I had the opportunity to address the Financial Stability Oversight Council (FSOC) chaired by Secretary Geithner to give them an overview of CIGFO and our roles and responsibilities. I emphasized that while CIGFO has authority to oversee the activities of FSOC, we can also be a valuable resource for objective assessment of the current regulatory structure. For example, CIGFO membership includes all the Inspectors General that have responsibility to conduct reviews of failed federally regulated banks. This body of work has given us considerable insight into the most common systemic weaknesses in managing risk that led to the failure of so many of these institutions as well as supervisory weaknesses on the part of the federal regulators.

Dodd-Frank also established the Consumer Financial Protection Bureau (CFPB). Although the Federal Reserve Board OIG has authority for oversight of CFPB, Dodd-Frank stipulates that until a Director is confirmed, the Treasury Secretary is responsible for the activities of the CFPB. We have been working jointly with the Federal Reserve Board OIG to perform ongoing oversight of Treasury's efforts to stand up this new bureau.

On September 27, 2010, the President signed into law the Small Business Jobs Act which created within Treasury the $30 billion Small Business Lending Fund (SBLF) and the $1.5 billion State Small Business Credit Initiative. My office is responsible for the oversight of these two programs. As required by the Act, I appointed a Special Deputy for SBLF Oversight, who reports directly to me, and she has begun to hire staff and initiate audits of SBLF.

Recently, Treasury announced that it would start to sell off its remaining $142 billion Fannie Mae and Freddie Mac mortgage-backed securities portfolio. We will be conducting oversight of this activity as well as other financial assistance provided through Treasury to Fannie Mae and Freddie Mac.

We continue to meet our mandate to perform reviews of all failed Treasury regulated institutions. While the rate of bank failures has slowed, we still have a substantial inventory of these reviews in process. We will also continue conducting our proactive audits and investigations of the American Recovery and Reinvestment Act (Recovery Act) recipients. To date, in Treasury's two major Recovery Act programs, Low Income Housing and Specified Energy Properties, Treasury has disbursed over $10 billion. Our focus initially has been on the Specified Energy Properties program. So far, we have initiated reviews of 60 Recovery Act payment recipients.

Furthermore, I am pleased to report that during this Semiannual period, we entered into a memorandum of understanding with the Office of the Comptroller of the Currency, Treasury's national bank regulator. The memorandum of understanding ensures that our office will have the necessary access to information and personnel during the conduct of an investigation or inquiry involving bank fraud that falls under our jurisdiction. Such access is absolutely critical so that my office can fully exercise its oversight responsibility for the integrity of the bank supervision process.

Since the beginning of the financial crisis, Treasury has continued to play a major role in the federal government's efforts to help stabilize the financial system and get the economy growing again. Treasury has been given an ever growing list of new programs and responsibilities to administer. We will continue to prioritize our resources in order to provide effective oversight to the most significant and highest risk Treasury programs and operations under our jurisdiction.

Eric M. Thorson
Inspector General

Contents

Office of Inspector General Overview

The Department of the Treasury's Office of Inspector General (OIG) was established pursuant to the 1988 amendments to the Inspector General Act of 1978. OIG is headed by an Inspector General appointed by the President, with the advice and consent of the Senate. Serving with the Inspector General in the immediate office is a Deputy Inspector General.

OIG performs independent, objective reviews of Treasury programs and operations, except for those of the Internal Revenue Service (IRS) and the Troubled Asset Relief Program (TARP), and keeps the Secretary of the Treasury and Congress fully informed of problems, deficiencies, and the need for corrective action. The Treasury Inspector General for Tax Administration (TIGTA) performs oversight related to IRS. A Special Inspector General and the Government Accountability Office perform oversight related to TARP.

OIG has five components: (1) Office of Audit, (2) Office of Investigations, (3) Office of Small Business Lending Fund (SBLF) Program Oversight; (4) Office of Counsel, and (5) Office of Management. OIG is headquartered in Washington, DC, and has an audit office in Boston, Massachusetts.

The Office of Audit, under the leadership of the Assistant Inspector General for Audit, performs and supervises audits, attestation engagements, and evaluations. The Assistant Inspector General for Audit has two deputies. One is primarily responsible for performance audits, and the other is primarily responsible for financial management, information technology, and financial assistance audits.

The Office of Investigations, under the leadership of the Assistant Inspector General for Investigations, performs investigations and conducts initiatives to detect and prevent fraud, waste, and abuse in Treasury programs and operations under our jurisdiction. It also manages the Treasury OIG Hotline to facilitate reporting of allegations involving Treasury programs and activities.

The Office of SBLF Program Oversight, under the leadership of a Special Deputy Inspector General, conducts, supervises, and coordinates audits and investigations of the SBLF program and State Small Business Credit Initiative (SSBCI).

The Office of Counsel, under the leadership of the Counsel to the Inspector General, provides legal advice to the Inspector General and all OIG components. The office represents the OIG in all legal proceedings and provides a variety of legal services including (1) processing all Freedom of Information Act and *Giglio* requests; (2) conducting ethics training; (3) ensuring compliance with financial disclosure requirements; (4) reviewing proposed legislation and regulations; (5) reviewing administrative subpoena requests; and (6) preparing for the Inspector General's signature, cease and desist letters to be sent to persons and entities misusing the Treasury seal and name.

The Office of Management, under the leadership of the Assistant Inspector General for Management, provides services to maintain the OIG administrative infrastructure.

As of March 31, 2011, OIG had 158 full-time staff. OIG's fiscal year 2011 appropriation is $29.6 million.

Treasury's Management and Performance Challenges

In accordance with the Reports Consolidation Act of 2000, the Treasury Inspector General annually provides the Secretary of the Treasury with his perspective on the most serious management and performance challenges facing the Department. In a memorandum to Secretary Geithner dated October 22, 2010, Inspector General Thorson reported four management and performance challenges. The following is an abridged version of that memorandum.

Transformation of Financial Regulation

Congress passed the Dodd-Frank Wall Street Reform and Consumer Protection Act (Dodd-Frank) in July 2010. The Dodd-Frank Act established a number of new responsibilities for Treasury.

Among those near term responsibilities and related challenges is Treasury's role in standing up the Consumer Financial Protection Bureau (CFPB). Eventually, when a director is confirmed, CFPB will become an independent bureau of the Board of Governors of the Federal Reserve System (FRB). In the interim, Treasury is charged with supporting the creation and management of it. Accordingly, while CFPB remains in Treasury, it will be subject to our audit and investigative oversight. Furthermore, during the interim, it should also be noted that we are coordinating those oversight efforts with the FRB OIG.

The Dodd-Frank Act also established the Financial Stability Oversight Council (FSOC), and the Council of Inspectors General on Financial Oversight (CIGFO). The mission of FSOC, which is chaired by the Treasury Secretary, is to identify risks to financial stability that could arise from the activities of large, interconnected financial companies; respond to any emerging threats to the financial system; and promote market discipline. CIGFO, which is chaired by the Treasury Inspector General, facilitates information sharing among inspectors general with a focus on reporting concerns that may apply to the broader financial sector and ways to improve financial oversight. CIGFO may also vote to convene a working group to evaluate the effectiveness and internal operations of FSOC.

The Dodd-Frank Act established two new offices within Treasury: The Office of Financial Research and the Federal Insurance Office. The Office of Financial Research is to be a data collection, research, and analysis arm of FSOC. The Federal Insurance Office is to monitor the insurance industry, including identifying gaps or issues in the regulation of insurance that could contribute to a systemic crisis in the insurance industry or financial system.

Intended to streamline the supervision of depository institutions and holding companies, the Dodd-Frank Act requires the transfer of the powers and duties of the Office of Thrift Supervision (OTS) to the Office of the Comptroller of the Currency (OCC), FRB, and the Federal Deposit Insurance Corporation (FDIC) no later than July 2011. Our office, FDIC OIG, and FRB OIG are required to jointly oversee and periodically report on the transfer of OTS functions.

Clearly, the intention of the Dodd-Frank Act is most notably to prevent, or at least minimize, the impact of a future financial sector crisis on the U.S. economy. In order to accomplish this, the act has placed a great deal of responsibility within Treasury and on the Treasury Secretary. The management challenge from our perspective is to implement an effective FSOC process supported by the newly created offices within Treasury and the streamlined banking regulatory structure that timely identifies and strongly responds to emerging risks. This is especially important in times of economic growth and financial institution profitability when such government action is likely to be unpopular. Our work plans will include reviews of Treasury's effectiveness in establishing the new offices and its other critical roles.

The other regulatory challenges that we previously reported remain. Specifically, since September 2007, and as of October 22, 2010, 93 Treasury-regulated financial institutions have failed, with estimated losses to the Deposit Insurance Fund (DIF) of approximately $36 billion.[1] Although many factors contributed to the turmoil in the financial markets, our work found that OCC and OTS did not identify early or force timely correction of unsafe and unsound practices by institutions under their supervision. The irresponsible lending practices of many institutions are now well-recognized— including reliance on risky products, such as option adjustable rate mortgages, and the degradation of underwriting standards. At the same time, financial institutions engaged in other high-risk activities, including high asset concentrations in commercial real estate and overreliance on unpredictable brokered deposits to fund rapid growth.

---

[1] As of March 31, 2011, 101 Treasury-regulated financial institutions have failed since September 2007 with total estimated losses to the DIF of approximately $36.6 billion.

Management of Treasury's Authorities Intended to Support and Improve the Economy

Congress provided Treasury with broad authorities to address the financial crisis under the Housing and Economic Recovery Act and the Emergency Economic Stabilization Act, both enacted in 2008, the American Recovery and Reinvestment Act of 2009 (Recovery Act), and the Small Business Jobs Act of 2010. Certain authorities in the Housing and Economic Recovery Act and Emergency Economic Stabilization Act have expired, but challenges remain in managing Treasury's outstanding investments. To an extent, Treasury's program administration under these two acts has matured. In contrast, program administration for the Recovery Act is evolving, and the Small Business Jobs Act programs must be stood up. The following discussion begins with the most recent act passed to support and improve the economy and moves on to the other new programs for which Treasury is responsible.

Management of the Small Business Lending Fund and State Small Business Credit Initiative

In September 2010, Congress enacted the Small Business Jobs Act. It created within Treasury the $30 billion SBLF and provided $1.5 billion to be allocated by Treasury to states for eligible state programs through the SSBCI. The act is intended to increase lending to small business and thereby support job creation. The challenge for Treasury will be to get these two programs up and running quickly while maintaining proper control to ensure transparency, equitable treatment of all participants, and achieving program results.

Under SBLF, in consultation with the regulator, Treasury will make capital investments in eligible financial institutions. Under certain conditions, eligible institutions can refinance securities issued under TARP's Capital Purchase Program. During the first 4½ years of Treasury's SBLF investment, participating institutions will pay dividends to Treasury of 5 percent, but that rate may be reduced to 1 percent. After 4½ years, the dividend rate increases to 9 percent and Treasury is to be repaid within 10 years.

It is important that a strong control structure with commensurate staffing be provided on the front end of this effort. It is also critical in setting up this program that Treasury build on its experience with the Capital Purchase Program. Furthermore, Treasury and regulators must coordinate to ensure that participating institutions comply with the terms and conditions of the investments, to include validation of increased small business lending in return for reduced dividend rates on Treasury investments.

Treasury has announced individual SSBCI funding allocations totaling $1.5 billion for the 50 states, the District of Columbia, and U.S. territories, intended to support new small business lending through local programs.

Management of Recovery Act Programs

Treasury is responsible for overseeing an estimated $150 billion of Recovery Act funding and tax relief. Treasury's specific Recovery Act program activities include grants for specified energy property in lieu of tax credits, grants to states for low-income housing projects in lieu of tax credits, Community Development Financial Institutions Fund grants and tax credits, economic recovery payments to social security

beneficiaries and others, and payments to U.S. territories for distribution to their citizens.

Many of these programs were new to Treasury in 2009. It is estimated that Treasury's Recovery Act payments in lieu of tax credit programs—for specified energy property and to states for low-income housing projects—will cost more than $20 billion. As of October 22, 2010, Treasury has awarded more than $6 billion under these programs and has yet to implement comprehensive monitoring procedures.[2] In 2009, we reported that Treasury dedicated only a small number of staff to award and monitor these funds. That has not changed and our concerns remain.

Management of the Housing and Economic Recovery Act and the Emergency Economic Stabilization Act

Under the Housing and Economic Recovery Act, Treasury continues to address the financial condition of Fannie Mae and Freddie Mac which are under the conservatorship of the Federal Housing Finance Agency. To cover the losses of the two entities and to maintain their positive net worth, Treasury purchased senior preferred stock in Fannie Mae and Freddie Mac. As reported in our memorandum, as of June 30, 2010, Treasury purchased $145 billion of senior preferred stock in the two entities. Treasury also purchased and is still holding $184 billion of mortgage-backed securities issued by Fannie Mae and Freddie Mac under a temporary purchase program that expired in December

---

[2] As of March 31, 2011, Treasury has awarded more than $10 billion under the payments in lieu of tax credit programs.

2009.[3] Even with this assistance, both entities remain in a weakened financial condition and may require prolonged assistance.

TARP, established under the Emergency Economic Stabilization Act, gave Treasury the authorities intended to bolster credit availability and address other serious problems in the domestic and world financial markets. Through its TARP programs, Treasury purchased direct loans and equity investments in many large financial institutions and other businesses, and guaranteed other troubled mortgage-related and financial assets. On October 3, 2010, the authority to make new investments under the TARP program expired. Treasury will, however, continue making payments for programs with existing contracts and commitments. TARP is expected to be less costly than first thought. As of the date of the memorandum, Treasury was estimating that the total cost of TARP would be about $50 billion. As the life-cycle of TARP matures and winds down, Treasury must now focus on managing and exiting from its TARP investments.

Anti-Money Laundering and Terrorist Financing/Bank Secrecy Act Enforcement

Treasury faces unique challenges in carrying out its responsibilities under the Bank Secrecy Act (BSA) and USA Patriot Act to prevent and detect money laundering and terrorist financing. The Financial Crimes Enforcement Network (FinCEN) is the Treasury bureau responsible for administering BSA. However, a large number of other federal and state entities

---

[3] As of March 31, 2011, Treasury purchased $156 billion of senior preferred stock and held $142 billion of mortgaged-backed securities in Fannie Mae and Freddie Mac.

participate in efforts to ensure compliance with BSA, including the five federal banking regulators, IRS, the Securities and Exchange Commission, the Department of Justice, and state regulators. Many of these entities also participate in efforts to ensure compliance with U.S. foreign sanctions programs administered by Treasury's Office of Foreign Assets Control. Accordingly, Treasury must coordinate the efforts of these multiple entities. To this end, FinCEN and the Office of Foreign Assets Control have entered into memoranda of understanding with many federal and state regulators in an attempt to build a consistent and effective process. While these memoranda promote coordination and cooperation, they are nonbinding and carry no penalties for violations. Furthermore, the USA Patriot Act has increased the types of financial institutions required to file BSA reports. In fiscal year 2009, financial institutions filed approximately 15 million BSA reports. FinCEN needs to work with regulators to ensure that financial institutions establish effective BSA compliance programs and file BSA reports, as required.

Adding to this risk is that financial institutions and their regulators may have decreased their attention to BSA and Office of Foreign Assets Control program compliance as they focus more on safety and soundness concerns during the current economic crisis.

FinCEN also has a particularly difficult challenge in dealing with money services businesses (MSB). Since IRS serves as the examining agency for MSBs, FinCEN has been working with IRS to ensure MSBs comply with BSA requirements. However, IRS does not have the resources necessary to annually inspect all MSBs or to identify unregistered MSBs, estimated to be in the tens of thousands. Within this context, FinCEN has been concerned with

MSBs that use informal value transfer systems and with those that issue, redeem, or sell prepaid (or stored value) cards.

In September 2010, to add transparency to possible illicit wire transfer use of the financial system, FinCEN proposed a regulatory requirement for certain depository institutions and MSBs to report cross-border electronic transmittals of funds. The purpose is to establish a centralized database to assist law enforcement in detecting transnational organized crime, multinational drug cartels, terrorist financing, and international tax evasion. If this proposal is implemented, ensuring that financial institutions comply with the cross-border electronic transmittals of funds reporting requirements and managing the database will be a significant challenge.

Management of Capital Investments

Managing large capital investments, particularly information technology (IT) investments, is a difficult challenge for any organization, public or private. In prior years, we reported on a number of capital investment projects that had either failed or had serious problems. This year, we identified challenges in four ongoing investments, two of which were identified by the Office of Management and Budget (OMB) as high-risk projects.

Replacement of Telecommunications Platform

OMB rated Treasury's Information Technology Infrastructure Telecommunications investment, with an overall value of $3.7 billion, as high-risk. Treasury's Acting Chief Information Officer rated it as poorly performing.

Common Identity Management System

OMB identified Treasury's Consolidated Enterprise Identity Management system as a high-risk project. This system is a $147 million effort to implement the requirements of Homeland Security Presidential Directive 12. The system has also been identified as being more than $40 million over budget and significantly behind schedule.

Data Center Consolidation

OMB began the Federal Data Center Consolidation Initiative to consolidate the number of federal data centers. Treasury has over 60 data centers around the country. Treasury plans to ultimately reduce the number of its data centers by 2015. This reduction would require Treasury to restructure its IT infrastructure over a relatively short time.

BSA IT Modernization

Treasury, through FinCEN, is undertaking a project known as BSA IT Modernization. Already underway, the project is expected to cost about $120 million. A prior attempt, from 2004 to 2006, to develop a new BSA system ended in failure with over $17 million wasted because of shortcomings in project planning, management, and oversight.

Treasury's decentralized management of IT investments presents a significant hurdle to the successful implementation of major department-wide and government-wide initiatives.

Office of Audit - Significant Audits and Other Products

Financial Management

Financial Audits

Consolidated Financial Statements

KPMG LLP, an independent public accountant, working under our supervision, issued an unqualified opinion on the Department's fiscal years 2010 and 2009 consolidated financial statements. The audit identified significant deficiencies related to (1) financial systems and reporting at IRS, (2) financial management practices at the Departmental level, (3) financial accounting and reporting at the Office of Financial Stability, and (4) information system controls at the Financial Management Service (FMS). The significant deficiency related to financial systems and reporting at IRS is considered a material weakness. KPMG LLP also reported that the Department's financial management systems did not substantially comply with the requirements of the Federal Financial Management Improvement Act of 1996 related to federal financial management system requirements and applicable federal accounting standards. In addition, the audit identified a reportable instance of noncompliance with laws and regulations related to section 6325[4] of the Internal Revenue Code. **(OIG-11-031)**

In connection with its audit of Treasury's consolidated financial statements, KPMG LLP issued a management letter that identified other matters involving internal control and Treasury operations related to (1) the compilation of the Department's consolidated financial statements, (2) the reconciliation of the Statement of Budgetary Resources to budget reports, (3) monitoring of Grants for Specified Energy Property in Lieu of Tax Credits, (4) service provider reviews, (5) financial reporting standards for Treasury's component entities, and (6) access controls. **(OIG-11-061)**

Other Financial Statement Audits

The Chief Financial Officers Act of 1990, as amended by the Government Management Reform Act of 1994, requires annual financial statement audits of Treasury and any component entities designated by OMB. In this regard, OMB designated IRS for annual financial statement audits. The financial statements of certain other Treasury component entities are audited pursuant to other requirements, their materiality to Treasury's consolidated financial statements, or as a management initiative.

---

[4] The Internal Revenue Code grants IRS the power to file a lien against the property of any taxpayer who neglects or refuses to pay all assessed federal taxes. Section 6325 requires IRS to release a federal tax lien within 30 days after the date the tax liability is satisfied, or has become legally unenforceable, or the Secretary of the Treasury has accepted a bond for the assessed tax.

The following table shows audit results for fiscal years 2010 and 2009.

Treasury-audited financial statements and related audits						
	Fiscal year 2010 audit results			Fiscal year 2009 audit results		
Entity	Opinion	Material weaknesses	Other significant deficiencies	Opinion	Material weaknesses	Other significant deficiencies
Government Management Reform Act/Chief Financial Officers Act requirements						
Department of the Treasury	UQ	1	3	UQ	2	2
Internal Revenue Service (A)	UQ	2	1	UQ	2	0
Other required audits						
Department of the Treasury's Special-Purpose Financial Statements	UQ	0	0	Q	1	0
Office of Financial Stability (TARP) (A)	UQ	0	1	UQ	0	2
Bureau of Engraving and Printing	UQ	0	0	UQ	0	0
Community Development Financial Institutions Fund	UQ	0	1	UQ	0	3
Office of DC Pensions	UQ	0	1	UQ	0	0
Exchange Stabilization Fund	UQ	0	1	UQ	0	1
Federal Financing Bank	UQ	0	0	UQ	0	0
Office of the Comptroller of the Currency	UQ	0	0	UQ	0	0
Office of Thrift Supervision	UQ	0	0	UQ	0	0
Treasury Forfeiture Fund	UQ	0	0	UQ	0	0
Mint						
Financial statements	UQ	0	0	UQ	0	0
Custodial gold and silver reserves	UQ	0	0	UQ	0	0
Other audited accounts that are material to Treasury financial statements						
Bureau of the Public Debt						
Schedule of Federal Debt (A)	UQ	0	0	UQ	0	0
Government trust funds	UQ	0	0	UQ	0	0
Financial Management Service						
Treasury-managed accounts	UQ	0	1	UQ	0	1
Operating cash of the federal government	UQ	0	1	UQ	0	1
Management-initiated audit						
Financial Crimes Enforcement Network	UQ	0	0	UQ	0	0
Alcohol and Tobacco Tax and Trade Bureau	UQ	1	0	UQ	2	0
UQ Unqualified opinion						
Q Qualified opinion due to omission of a required disclosure and misstatement of certain account balances in the financial statement notes						
(A) Audited by Government Accountability Office						

The fiscal year 2010 audits of Treasury's component entities and its special-purpose financial statements identified the following material weakness and other significant deficiencies. These audits were performed by KPMG LLP or other independent public accountants under our supervision.

Material Weakness

- The Alcohol and Tobacco Tax and Trade Bureau's controls over the review of purchase requisitions. **(OIG-11-051)**

Other Significant Deficiencies

- The Community Development Financial Institutions (CDFI) Fund's controls over accounting and investments. **(OIG-11-024)**

- The Office of D.C. Pensions' controls over annuitant payment processing. **(OIG-11-050)**

- The Exchange Stabilization Fund's controls over accounting for movements in foreign currency values for other foreign currency denominated

assets and investment securities. **(OIG-11-044)**

- FMS information technology controls over systems managed by FMS and third parties. **(OIG-11-034, OIG-11-037)**

In connection with the fiscal year 2010 financial statement audits, the auditors issued management letters on other matters involving internal control to the Bureau of Engraving and Printing **(OIG-11-020)**, CDFI Fund **(OIG-11-025)**, Federal Financing Bank **(OIG-11-022)**, Mint **(OIG-11-043)**, OCC **(OIG-11-046)**, and OTS **(OIG-11-053)**. In addition, the auditors issued two sensitive but unclassified management reports that detailed FMS's significant deficiency related to IT controls over systems managed by it and third parties and recommended corrective actions. **(OIG-11-035, OIG-11-038)**

The following instances of noncompliance with the Federal Financial Management Improvement Act of 1996, which all relate to IRS, were reported in connection with the audit of the Department's fiscal year 2010 consolidated financial statements.

Condition	Type of noncompliance
Persistent deficiencies in internal control over information security remain uncorrected. As a result of these deficiencies, IRS was (1) unable to rely upon these controls to provide reasonable assurance that its financial statements are fairly stated in the absence of effective compensating procedures, (2) unable to ensure the reliability of other financial management information produced by its systems, and (3) at increased risk of compromising confidential IRS and taxpayer information. (first reported in fiscal year 1997)	Federal financial management systems requirements
Automated systems for tax related transactions did not support the net taxes receivable amount on the balance sheet and other required supplemental information related to uncollected taxes–compliance assessments and tax write-offs– in accordance with Statement of Federal Financial Accounting Standards No. 7, *Accounting for Revenue and Other Financing Sources and Concepts for Reconciling Budgetary and Financial Accounting.* (first reported in fiscal year 1997)	Federal accounting standards

The status of these noncompliances, including progress in implementing remediation plans, will be evaluated as part of the audit of the Department's fiscal year 2011 consolidated financial statements.

Attestation Engagement

KPMG LLP, working under our supervision, issued an unqualified opinion that the Bureau of the Public Debt (BPD) Trust Fund Management Branch's assertions pertaining to the schedule of assets and liabilities and related schedule of activity of selected trust funds, as of and for the year ended September 30, 2010, are fairly stated. These schedules relate to the functions of the Trust Fund Management Branch as custodian of the Federal Supplementary Medical Insurance Trust Fund, Federal Hospital Insurance Trust Fund, Highway Trust Fund, Airport and Airway Trust Fund, Hazardous Substance Superfund Trust Fund, Leaking Underground Storage Tank Trust Fund, Oil Spill Liability Trust Fund, Harbor Maintenance Trust Fund, Inland Waterways Trust Fund, and South Dakota Terrestrial Wildlife Habitat Restoration Trust Fund. The attestation examination did not identify any significant deficiencies in internal control or instances of reportable noncompliance with laws and regulations. **(OIG-11-017)**

Information Technology

Fiscal Year 2010 Audit of Treasury's Federal Information Security Management Act Implementation for Its Unclassified Systems

The Federal Information Security Management Act (FISMA) requires each Inspector General to perform an annual, independent evaluation of their agency's information security program and practices. We contracted with KPMG LLP to perform an audit of FISMA compliance for the Department's unclassified systems with the exception of IRS. TIGTA performed the annual evaluation for IRS. Based on the results reported by KPMG LLP and TIGTA, we determined that Treasury's information security program was in place and was generally consistent with FISMA.

However, the KPMG LLP audit of Treasury's unclassified systems (except for those of IRS) found that additional steps are required to ensure that Treasury's information security risk management program and practices fully comply with applicable National Institute of Standards and Technology standards and guidelines and FISMA requirements. Specifically, (1) account management activities were not consistently performed as required by Treasury's directive on information security, (2) outsourcing the Information System Security Officer role created an IT governance concern at FMS, (3) plans of actions and milestones were not updated timely and maintained at FMS and OCC, (4) security incidents were not reported timely at BPD and the Alcohol and Tobacco Tax and Trade Bureau, (5) reviews of audit logs were not documented at BEP, (6) the electronic media destruction process at FinCEN was not fully compliant with its internal policies, and (7) password settings were not properly configured to lockout for a BPD system.

TIGTA reported that IRS was also generally consistent with FISMA requirements. However, TIGTA noted that the IRS information security program was not fully effective as a result of the conditions identified in configuration management, security training, plans of action and milestones, identity and access management, continuous monitoring management, contingency planning, and contractor systems.

In addition, the General Accountability Office (GAO) reported a continuing material weakness in IRS's internal control over information security that resulted in IRS's inability to rely on the controls embedded in its automated financial management systems. **(OIG-11-023)**

Fiscal Year 2010 Audit of Treasury's FISMA Implementation for Its Collateral National Security Systems

We performed the fiscal year 2010 audit of Treasury's FISMA implementation for its collateral national security systems, excluding IRS systems. We found that Treasury's information security program and practices for Treasury's non-IRS collateral national security systems are generally consistent with FISMA requirements but that improvements can enhance its security program. Management agreed with our findings and recommendations. Due to the sensitive nature of these systems, this report has been designated Sensitive But Unclassified. **(OIG-11-005)**

Treasury is Generally in Compliance with the Executive Order on Computer Software Piracy

Executive Order 13103, Computer Software Piracy, directs executive agencies to work diligently to prevent and combat computer software piracy and to ensure that their policies, procedures, and practices are adequate and fully implement the executive order.

We determined that the Department was generally in compliance with Executive Order 13103, but that policy and procedures could be improved to ensure compliance. Management agreed with our findings and recommendations.
(OIG-11-036)

Programs and Operations

Failed Bank Reviews

OCC and OTS regulate and supervise most of the nation's largest banks and thrifts. OCC regulates national chartered banks, and OTS regulates thrifts.[5]

In 1991, Congress enacted the Federal Deposit Insurance Corporation Improvement Act (FDICIA). The law was enacted following the failures of about a thousand banks and thrifts from 1986 to 1990. Amendments to FDICIA included the addition of Section 38, Prompt Corrective Action, which requires federal banking agencies to take specific supervisory actions in response to certain circumstances.[6]

Section 38 of FDICIA also requires the Inspector General for the primary federal regulator of a failed financial institution conduct a material loss review (MLR) when the estimated loss to the DIF is "material." An MLR requires that we determine the causes of the failure and assess the supervision of the institution, including the implementation of the Section 38 prompt corrective action provisions. Section 38 as amended by the Dodd-Frank Act, defines a material loss as a loss to the DIF that exceeds $200 million for 2010 and 2011, $150

---

[5] Pursuant to Dodd-Frank, the functions of OTS are to be transferred to other federal banking agencies, including OCC, on July 21, 2011, and OTS is to be abolished.

[6] Prompt corrective action is a framework of supervisory actions for insured institutions that are not adequately capitalized. It was intended to ensure that action is taken when an institution becomes financially troubled in order to prevent a failure or minimize resulting losses. These actions become increasingly more severe as the institution falls into lower capital categories. The capital categories are well-capitalized, adequately capitalized, undercapitalized, significantly undercapitalized, and critically undercapitalized.

million for 2012 and 2013, and $50 million for 2014 and thereafter (with a provision to temporarily raise the threshold to $75 million in certain circumstances). Section 38 also requires a review of all bank failures with losses under those threshold amounts for the purposes of (1) ascertaining the grounds identified by OCC or OTS for appointing FDIC as receiver and (2) determining whether any unusual circumstances exist that might warrant a more in-depth review of the loss. This provision applies to bank failures from October 1, 2009, forward.[7]

From the beginning of the current economic crisis in 2007 through March 31, 2011, FDIC and other banking regulators closed more than 350 banks and thrifts. Treasury was responsible for regulating 101 of those institutions. Of the 101 failures, 53 resulted in a material loss to the DIF. In prior semiannual reports, we reported on 21 MLRs completed during the current crisis. During this semiannual reporting period, we did not complete any MLRs due to other priority work, including reviews related to the transfer of OTS functions and Treasury's activities to stand up the CFPB. Accordingly, as of the end of the reporting period, we still have 32 MLRs in progress. We are striving to complete these during calendar year 2011.

As previously reported, from those MLRs that we have completed, we have seen a number of trends emerge. With respect to the causes of institution's failures, we found poor underwriting and overly aggressive growth strategies fueled by volatile and costly wholesale

funding (e.g., brokered deposits, Federal Home Loan Bank loans); risky lending products such as option adjustable rate mortgages; high asset concentrations; and inadequate risk management systems. In addition, the management and boards of these institutions were often ineffective. The economic recession and the decline in the real estate market were also factors in most of the failures.

With respect to OCC's and OTS's supervision, we found that both regulators conducted regular and timely examinations and identified operational problems, but were slow to take timely and effective enforcement action. We also found that in assessing these institutions, examiners regularly gave too much weight to profitability and performing loans and not enough to the amount of risk these institutions had taken on. We also noted that regulators took the appropriate prompt corrective actions when warranted but those actions did not prevent a material loss to the DIF. We, with the FDIC OIG, are currently examining the general effectiveness of the prompt corrective action provisions of FDICIA.

Nonmaterial Loss Reviews

During this semiannual reporting period, 11 OCC- or OTS-regulated financial institutions failed with losses below $200 million, the current threshold triggering an MLR. Our required determinations as to whether any unusual circumstances exist warranting a more in-depth review of the loss of any of these institutions is provided in the "Bank Failures and Nonmaterial Loss Reviews" section of this report. With the exception of 1 of the 11 institutions, we determined that there were no unusual circumstances surrounding the failures or the supervision exercised by OTS and OCC, so a more in-depth review of the failures by our office was not warranted.

---

[7] Prior to the Dodd-Frank Act, an MLR was required if loss to the DIF from a bank failure exceeded the greater of $25 million or 2 percent of the institution's total assets. There was also no requirement for us to review bank failures with losses less than this threshold.

During the period, we issued 32 final audit reports on our nonmaterial loss reviews, consisting of 25 final audit reports on institutions that failed in the prior semiannual reporting period and 7 final audit reports on institutions that failed during this semiannual reporting period. A list of these final audit reports is provided in the Statistical Summary section of this report. As of March 31, 2011, we had 4 nonmaterial audit reports in progress.

Other Performance Audits

Review of the Joint Implementation Plan for the Transfer of Office of Thrift Supervision Functions

We conducted a review with the FDIC OIG and FRB OIG of the Joint Implementation Plan prepared by the Board, FDIC, OCC, and OTS. The Plan details the steps the federal banking agencies will take to implement the provisions of Title III, *Transfer of Powers to the Comptroller of the Currency, the Corporation, and the Board of Governors,* of Dodd-Frank. Section 327 of Title III mandated the preparation of the Plan and our offices' review.

The objective of our review, as defined by section 327, was to determine whether the Plan conforms to the provisions of sections 301 through 326 of Title III, to include determining whether it (1) sufficiently takes into consideration the orderly transfer of personnel, (2) describes procedures and safeguards to ensure that OTS employees are not unfairly disadvantaged relative to employees of OCC and FDIC, (3) sufficiently takes into consideration the orderly transfer of authority and responsibilities, (4) sufficiently takes into consideration the effective transfer of funds, and (5) sufficiently takes into consideration the orderly transfer of property. As appropriate, we

were also to provide any additional recommendations for an orderly and effective process.

We concluded that the Plan generally conforms to the provisions of sections 301 through 326 of Title III. However, we did report on an omission in the Plan. Specifically, the Plan does not address the prohibition against involuntary separation or relocation of transferred OTS employees for 30 months (except under certain circumstances). The principals agreed with our recommendation to amend the Plan to address this requirement.

We also reported that, while not impacting our overall conclusion on the Plan, certain details need to be worked out to ensure that OTS employees are not unfairly disadvantaged and an orderly transfer of OTS powers, authority, and employees can be effectively accomplished. For example, neither the number of employees to be transferred to OCC nor the assignment of functions for those employees had been finalized. In addition, OTS officials expressed concerns relating to (1) OCC's assignment of individual employees and (2) additional OCC certification requirements and a newly created pay band for certain transferring OTS examiners. Finally, we reported on several other matters associated with the transfer of OTS functions, including an OTS pension fund, savings association assessments, and financial reporting by OTS. **(OIG-11-064)**

The Failed and Costly BSA Direct Retrieval and Sharing (R&S) System Development Effort Provides Important Lessons for FinCEN's BSA Modernization Program

In 2004, FinCEN embarked on a major initiative, known as BSA Direct, to improve the usefulness and functionality of the BSA data and transition the BSA data from the IRS. As part of that effort, FinCEN awarded a contract to Electronic Data Systems Corporation to design, develop, implement, and provide web hosting and support for the retrieval and sharing component of the project, known as BSA Direct R&S. FinCEN terminated BSA Direct R&S in July 2006, after determining that the project had no guarantee of success. The total amount of funding expended on the failed project was $17.4 million.

Our audit concluded that the BSA Direct R&S failed for a number of reasons. The primary cause was poor project management. FinCEN allowed a personal services contractor who had no information technology experience, project management expertise, or authority, to usurp the duties of the project manager and contracting officer. Also, FinCEN did not properly (1) monitor the BSA Direct R&S development effort, (2) obtain proper security clearances for contractors, and (3) maintain contract records. FinCEN also did not report to Treasury's Office of Chief Information Officer (OCIO) on the status of the project and Treasury's OCIO did not actively oversee the project.

In addition to poor planning for BSA Direct R&S, FinCEN did not adequately coordinate with IRS or Treasury's OCIO to determine whether this system was duplicative of IRS's web-based Currency and Banking Retrieval System. FinCEN also did not coordinate with IRS to develop a strategy for managing BSA data and avoiding the duplication and added costs that occurred. Finally, FinCEN did not adequately determine functional requirements or user needs prior to awarding the contract.

By the time FinCEN terminated the contract in July 2006, it had spent $17.4 million on BSA

Direct R&S efforts, representing a significant escalation from the nearly $9 million contract initially awarded to Electronic Data Systems Corporation. To cover the additional contract and other costs of the project, FinCEN used funds from both the Treasury Forfeiture Fund and its fiscal years 2005 and 2006 appropriations. To ensure FinCEN's use of funds for the project were legal and appropriate, we requested an opinion from GAO. GAO concluded that FinCEN could legally draw on fiscal year 2003 and 2004 appropriations to fund BSA Direct R&S, but had improperly charged certain obligations to its fiscal year 2005 and 2006 appropriations in violation of the bona fide needs rule. (The bona fide needs rule provides that an appropriation or fund limited for obligation to a definite period is available only for payment of expenses properly incurred during the period of availability or to complete contracts properly made within that period of availability of the appropriation.) In accordance with GAO's conclusion, FinCEN adjusted its accounts and its 2004 and 2005 appropriations.

We recommended, that FinCEN (1) ensure that future system development projects, including its current BSA modernization project, are properly planned and the necessary expertise for project management is in place; (2) coordinate with Treasury's OCIO concerning the current BSA modernization project as well as any future information technology initiatives; (3) coordinate with IRS for a consolidated solution to meeting the data needs of its customers; (4) ensure that adequate contract and financial records are maintained for the current BSA modernization project to allow for audit and accurate reporting; and (6) assess the controls over its use of personal services contracts to ensure that such contracts are appropriate to its mission, and that individuals hired under personal services contracts perform duties that are appropriate and within their expertise. We also recommended that Treasury's OCIO closely monitor the current BSA modernization project to ensure that sound project management principles are followed.

In its written response, FinCEN stated that it has gone through many changes since the BSA Direct R&S effort, gained project management expertise, and is under new leadership. According to FinCEN, it has implemented a number of management tools and techniques to ensure successful implementation of the current BSA modernization program. FinCEN stated that the problems experienced with BSA Direct R&S are not reflective of the current program. FinCEN further noted that it routinely coordinates with Treasury OCIO, IRS, and OMB to ensure adequate oversight and planning for the program. It also has restricted the use of personal services contracts to situations where no other contractual vehicle is possible. In fact, FinCEN stated that it currently has no personal services contract and does not anticipate one in the future.

An official with Treasury's OCIO stated in a written response that the office is closely monitoring major information technology investments including the current BSA modernization program.

It is important to note that FinCEN's senior management team has changed since the BSA Direct R&S project was terminated and as we noted in our report, it is not our intent to imply that the problems experienced with BSA Direct R&S project are reflective of the current BSA IT modernization effort. That said, we currently have an audit underway to assess BSA IT modernization. **(OIG-11-057)**

Other Reviews

Treasury's Activities to Establish the Consumer Financial Protection Bureau

Title X of the Dodd-Frank Act established CFPB as an independent bureau within the FRB. The Secretary of the Treasury has the authority to conduct certain interim activities related to CFPB's establishment and exercise certain bureau authorities until a CFPB Director is confirmed by the Senate. On November 22, 2010, Inspector General Thorson and FRB Inspector General Coleman each received a request from the then Ranking Members of the House Committee on Financial Services and its Subcommittee on Oversight and Investigation asking that we affirm our respective offices' oversight role of CFPB until the bureau transfers to the FRB. The requests also asked that we provide information on a number of other matters related to transparency, CFPB's organizational structure, and CFPB's regulatory agenda by January 10, 2011.

In preparing our response, we and the FRB OIG jointly (1) reviewed the applicable sections of the Dodd-Frank Act and other relevant laws and (2) requested, obtained, and reviewed relevant information and documentation from Treasury and FRB. In addition, we interviewed key Treasury officials including Professor Elizabeth Warren, Assistant to the President and Special Advisor to the Secretary of the Treasury on the CFPB; Treasury's General Counsel; the Chief of Staff of the CFPB Implementation Team; and others. We and the FRB OIG provided our joint response to the Chairmen and Ranking Members dated January 10, 2011. **(OIG-CA-11-004)**

We and the FRB OIG plan to continue providing joint oversight of CFPB until such

time as the bureau transfers to the FRB and a
CFPB Director is confirmed.

Office of Investigations - Significant Investigations

Indictment and Sentencing in Fraudulent Check Scheme

BPD informed our office that an individual in New Bern, North Carolina, was creating and passing fraudulent checks totaling approximately $1 million. The individual attempted to withdraw the funds from BPD's Treasury Direct Program while utilizing a BPD bank routing number on each fraudulent check. Treasury Direct is a web-based system that allows investors to purchase a full range of Treasury securities through an online account.

As a result of our investigation, the individual was indicted in federal court during October 2010 on 16 counts of wire, bank, and mail fraud violations. On March 14, 2011, the individual appeared in U.S. District Court, Raleigh, North Carolina, and pled guilty to 1 count of bank fraud. Sentencing is scheduled for June 13, 2011.

Individual Indicted in Fraudulent Tax Refund Scheme Utilizing Treasury Direct Accounts

BPD informed our office of a possible multi-million dollar IRS tax refund scheme involving multiple subjects. The scheme involved opening BPD Treasury Direct accounts with false identities and purchasing Treasury bonds/securities with fraudulent tax refunds deposited into those accounts.

In December 2010, OIG special agents executed a Federal arrest warrant on a subject in this scheme attempting to flee the country from the Dulles International Airport, Dulles, Virginia. In January 2011, the arrested individual was indicted by the U.S. District Court in the Northern District of Texas for Conspiracy to Steal Government Funds. Additionally, the U.S. Attorney's Office issued seizure warrants for five fraudulent Treasury Direct accounts which resulted in the recovery of over $781,000. Further judicial action is pending.

Check Forgery Insurance Fund Initiative

The Office of Investigations is currently involved in a joint initiative with FMS in an effort to combat Treasury check fraud. This initiative's primary focus is the Check Forgery Insurance Fund. The Fund, established in 1941, is a revolving fund administered by FMS to settle claims of non-receipt of U.S. Treasury checks. The purpose of the Fund is to ensure that the intended payees, whose checks were fraudulently negotiated, receive settlement in a timely manner. Since this initiative began in August 2010, we have identified thousands of investigative leads associated with the Fund. The following cases highlight some of our Fund investigations:

- In September 2010, we initiated an investigation regarding a stolen Treasury check in Maryland. The investigation determined that a Treasury check in the amount of $674 was stolen and negotiated by a subject who resided in Hyattsville, Maryland. Furthermore, the investigation revealed that the Treasury check was intended as Supplemental Security Income payment for a disabled child, who was on a ventilator because of a debilitating illness. We obtained and executed a Maryland State arrest warrant which charged the subject with numerous violations related to the theft of the Treasury check. In January 2011, the subject pled guilty to misdemeanor theft in Prince George's County District Court and was sentenced to 90 days incarceration, with 89 days suspended and credit for a day as time served. In addition, the subject was placed on unsupervised probation for 1 year and ordered to pay restitution to the victim.

- In November 2010, we initiated an investigation into the theft and subsequent deposit of a stolen Treasury check. Our investigation substantiated that the subject stole the check from the mail, deposited it into his personal checking account, and then withdrew the money for personal use. Felony charges for theft, forgery, and issuing a false document were subsequently filed in Anne Arundel County, Maryland. In February 2011, the subject appeared in court and entered a guilty plea, and was sentenced to 1 year of supervised probation and ordered to pay $100 in fines and court costs.

- In December 2010, based on information provided by FMS, we initiated an investigation against a claimant who maintained that she had never received or negotiated a Treasury check made out to her name in the amount of $4,443. Our investigation determined that the claimant filed a false claim with FMS. She was subsequently charged in the District Court for Baltimore City, Maryland, with 1 count of felony theft. Judicial action is still pending.

Guilty Plea in Mint Procurement Fraud

We received an allegation from the Mint that an employee engaged in the steering of small purchases of supplies totaling hundreds of thousands of dollars to a company, owned by a former Mint employee, in which the employee had a financial interest. The subject used two methods to direct the Mint to buy supplies from the company. One was through the use of a government-issued credit card, and the other was through a requisition process whereby the employee submitted requisitions that contained false representations that the Mint had a blanket purchase agreement with the company for the purchase of office supplies. The employee structured the purchases in the amount of $4,999 (which is one dollar less than the single purchase limit) to avoid a competitive bidding process.

In February 2011, the employee pled guilty in U.S. District for the Eastern District of Pennsylvania to five counts of mail fraud; five counts of wire fraud; five counts of conflict of interest; and four counts of making false statements. Sentencing is scheduled for May 26, 2011, at which time the employee faces up to 245 years imprisonment and $4.7 million in penalties.

Conviction in OCC Burglary Investigation

OCC's field office in Charlotte, North Carolina, was burglarized and an OCC laptop computer was stolen. OIG special agents identified and interviewed a suspect who was in the custody of the Charlotte-Mecklenburg, North Carolina, Police Department on unrelated theft charges. The suspect subsequently admitted to entering the OCC office space unlawfully and stealing the laptop computer.

In January 2011, the suspect was found guilty on North Carolina state burglary and theft violations related to the OCC theft. His conviction served as the requisite predicate offense for him to be sentenced under the state's habitual offender felony statute. Based upon the combination of this conviction, along with his previous convictions, the subject was sentenced to an incarceration of 20 to 24 years.

Suspect Surrenders in Fraud for Services Investigation

A joint investigation with the General Services Administration OIG and the Washington Metropolitan Police Department resulted in an individual surrendering after agents conducted a search at locations frequented by the suspect. The individual allegedly defrauded a real estate leasing company, located in Washington, D.C., by entering into a 1 year lease for office space by representing himself as being on the General Services Administration Multiple Award Schedule and a contractor for the Treasury Department. The investigation confirmed that he was neither on the General Services Administration Multiple Award Schedule nor a Treasury contractor. Subsequently, the individual turned himself in to authorities at the Washington, D.C., Superior Court pursuant to an outstanding felony arrest warrant for first degree theft.

Subject Pled Guilty and Sentenced for Theft From the Mint

We initiated an investigation based on information received from the Mint regarding the possible compromise of customers' credit card numbers by an employee of a Mint contractor. The investigation, which included a search warrant executed on the contractor employee's residence, revealed that the individual fraudulently purchased commemorative coins from the Mint using the credit card numbers of a Mint customer.

In February 2011, the contract employee pled guilty to theft in Marion County, Indiana, and was sentenced to 1 year probation, and ordered to pay restitution to the Mint. In addition, the employee was terminated.

Supervisory Special Agent Indicted for Defrauding the Government

An investigation by our office determined that an OIG Supervisory Special Agent, who was also a U.S. Marine Corps Reserve Officer, knowingly and willfully defrauded the government of salary, leave, retirement, and other benefits from his civilian employment between May and October 2007 to which he was not entitled because he was in an active military duty status.

The supervisory special agent was indicted by a federal grand jury for embezzlement, wire fraud, and false statements related to the theft of pay and benefits from the Treasury Department. He was subsequently arrested and taken into custody at his residence. In October 2010, the supervisory special agent entered into a deferred prosecution agreement whereby he admitted to and acknowledged his guilt, agreed to pay restitution in the amount of $35,791, and resigned from federal service.

OCC Examiner Admits Misusing Government Travel Card

In November 2010, OCC informed us that a national bank examiner may have misused her government travel card on multiple occasions in 2009 and 2010 to obtain cash advances while not on travel status, as well as cash advances that exceeded reasonable amounts.

The investigation resulted in the examiner admitting that she had used cash advances inappropriately. Our report of investigation was referred to OCC for administrative action.

Negligent Discharge of a Weapon by Mint Police Officer

An investigation by our office into a shooting incident at the Philadelphia, Pennsylvania, Mint facility determined that a Mint police officer accidentally shot himself in the upper rear left leg with a personally owned pistol. The officer violated multiple Treasury and Mint directives by possessing and discharging an unauthorized and unregistered firearm inside a Mint facility. This matter was declined for criminal prosecution by the U.S. Attorney's Office and the officer retired prior to administrative action by the Mint.

Following are updates to significant investigative activities reported in prior semiannual reports.

Acceptance of Gifts by OCC Examiner - Update

As previously reported, an investigation by our office determined that a national bank examiner violated the Employee Standards of Conduct by accepting gratuities in the form of golf fees. Although criminal prosecution was declined, the examiner was given a 30-day unpaid suspension for violating his ethical and professional responsibilities as a bank examiner.

Misuse of Government-Issued Badge and Credentials by an OCC Official - Update

As previously reported, an investigation by our office determined that an OCC official inappropriately presented his badge and credential to a local police officer and to a third party during a traffic incident. Although criminal prosecution was declined, the official was issued a notice of proposed suspension, prompting that official's resignation from the OCC in November 2010.

Mint Responds to Management Implication Report - Update

As previously reported, we issued a Management Implication Report to the Mint with four recommendations to improve the integrity of its Mutilated Coin Program. In February 2011, the Mint informed us that they concurred with all four recommendations to address vulnerabilities reported in our Management Implication Report. The Mint advised that they would implement numerous policy changes regarding the administrative handling of mutilated coins to include developing a standardized operating procedure to conduct inspections of incoming shipments at the melting facility, redeeming only mutilated coins, requiring additional information from individuals and companies redeeming mutilated coins prior to approving payment, and developing a legal certification on all forms used in the Mutilated Coin Program to discourage potential exploitation of the program.

Office of SBLF Program Oversight

Oversight of Small Business Lending Programs

On September 27, 2010, the President signed into law the Small Business Jobs Act of 2010 to help increase credit availability for small businesses. The act established the $30 billion SBLF to be used by Treasury to inject capital into small and medium banks with incentives to encourage them to increase their small business lending. It also created the SSBCI that provides Treasury with $1.5 billion to support state programs designed to increase access to credit for small businesses.

To ensure proper oversight of the SBLF, the act established the Office of SBLF Program Oversight within the Treasury OIG and directed that a Special Deputy Inspector General be appointed to lead the office. The Office is responsible for all audit and investigative activities relating to the SBLF program and for recommending program improvements. Congress also directed that the OIG audit participating states' uses of SSBCI funds, and required Treasury to recoup any misused funds identified by the OIG audits.

Building the Office of SBLF Program Oversight

In light of the importance of the small business lending initiatives to the nation's economic recovery, the OIG quickly stood up the Office of SBLF Program Oversight. A Special Deputy Inspector General was appointed on December 5, 2010, OIG auditors were detailed to the new Office so that work could begin immediately, and steps were taken to recruit and hire senior counsel, auditors, and analysts. We plan to use existing OIG investigative staff to

evaluate potential fraud vulnerabilities and to investigate allegations of fraud and abuse. Efforts are also underway to contract for external audit support to review the expenditure of SSBCI funds by state agencies.

Oversight Activities to Date

We view our oversight role both prospectively (to advise Treasury managers during program development on issues relating to internal controls and oversight) and retrospectively (to evaluate program effectiveness and the adequacy of Treasury's oversight activities). We also seek to promote transparency over Treasury's management and operation of the small business lending initiatives to ensure accountability and to investigate cases of fraud, waste, and abuse in the SBLF and SSBCI programs.

Although we are still building the Office of SBLF Program Oversight, we have been working to provide meaningful oversight and fraud prevention advice to Treasury officials to mitigate risks and to ensure that problems are identified and corrected early in program implementation. To this end, the Special Deputy Inspector General and her staff meet weekly with SBLF and SSBCI program directors and their staffs to discuss progress in program implementation, ongoing issues, and upcoming developments. They also communicate regularly with staff from Treasury's General Counsel to discuss legal and regulatory issues relating to the SBLF and SSBCI programs. With respect to specific activities and accomplishments during the semiannual period, the Office has:

- recommended that SBLF and SSBCI program terms and agreements contain oversight language acknowledging the jurisdiction and authority of the OIG to have access to participant records and loan files and to oversee program compliance;

- conducted a risk assessment of the small business lending initiatives to identify potential risks and vulnerabilities in program management and planning that could impede Treasury's ability to effectively oversee funded projects and meet statutory requirements;

- advised SBLF and SSBCI managers on the design of internal control;

- recommended that the SSBCI application form be modified to include questions that would allow Treasury officials to assess the capability of states to adequately oversee program requirements, and at Treasury's request, developed the recommended questions;

- worked collaboratively with SSBCI program managers to develop a matrix of SSBCI compliance requirements and a joint oversight strategy for the SSBCI program;

- initiated an audit of Treasury's investment decision process for SBLF funding and progress in implementing the program;

- participated in a Treasury-hosted webinar with state agencies on the SSBCI program to discuss the oversight role of the OIG and related plans for reviewing how states use allocated funds and oversee lender compliance with program requirements; and

- established lines of communication with GAO and the OIGs at FRB and FDIC

to coordinate audit and investigative plans.

Future Oversight Plans

To meet its responsibilities under the Act, the Office has developed a risk-based oversight plan for monitoring, evaluating, and reporting on Treasury's implementation of the SBLF and SSBCI programs. Risks were identified based on a review of program legislation and an examination of vulnerabilities in program management and planning. In developing the plan, the Office also considered reports of lessons learned from two TARP programs with similarities to SBLF—the Capital Purchase Program and Community Development Capital Initiative. Finally, congressional oversight committees were consulted on activities to target for oversight attention. Collectively these efforts identified several areas for audit attention. The areas identified within SBLF program include:

- refinancing of the Capital Purchase Program and Community Development Capital Initiative investments;

- eligibility determinations for matched funding;

- quality of loan underwriting by participating institutions;

- accuracy of small business lending gains supporting dividend rate reductions;

- use of funds by SBLF participants and the characteristics of institutions receiving funding; and

- program impact on small business lending and job creation.

Areas within the SSBCI program targeted for oversight will include:

- expenditure of funds allocated to states (as directed by the Small Business Jobs Act);

- adequacy of state oversight of program compliance requirements; and

- accuracy of state reporting of program accomplishments.

Other OIG Accomplishments and Activity

CIGIE Award Ceremony

Treasury OIG staff were recognized with three prestigious Awards for Excellence at the Annual Council of the Inspectors General on Integrity and Efficiency (CIGIE) Awards Ceremony held on October 19, 2010. Honored were:

- a high impact audit that identified OTS's involvement in the inappropriate backdating of capital contributions by six thrifts (Audit Award for Excellence);
- a joint FDIC OIG and Treasury OIG evaluation of the federal regulatory oversight of the failed Washington Mutual Bank; and
- the exceptional officewide coordination within Treasury OIG to quickly staff up the Office of Audit to perform mandated reviews of failed banks.

Pictured above are Marla Freedman, Assistant Inspector General for Audit; Kieu Rubb, Director, Procurement and Manufacturing Audit; Mike Maloney, Director, Fiscal Service Audit; Susan Barron, Director, Banking Audit; Bob Taylor, Deputy Assistant Inspector General for Audit; Dennis Schindel, Deputy Inspector General; and Joey Maranto, Director, Audit Operations.

European Delegation

On January 25, 2011, the Inspector General and senior management staff hosted a European delegation that was sponsored by the U.S. State Department as part of the International Visitor Leadership Program. The delegation included 16 visitors from both the public and private sector representing 16 European countries. We briefed the delegation on the mission, structure and activities of our office as well as the how the inspector general concept works throughout the U.S. Government.

Pictured above are OIG executives with members of the European delegation.

OIG Audit Leadership Roles

Treasury OIG's audit professionals actively support and serve on various important public and private professional organizations supporting the federal audit community. Examples of Treasury OIG Audit personnel participation in these organizations follow:

Marla Freedman, Assistant Inspector General for Audit, serves as co-chair of the Federal Audit Executive Council's Professional Development Committee which is actively involved in auditor training and development matters. **Bob Taylor**, Deputy Assistant Inspector General for Performance Audits, also serves on this committee. As a notable accomplishment during this semiannual reporting period, the Committee facilitated the reestablishment of an Introductory Auditor Training program for the Inspector General community, which is being sponsored by the Department of Education OIG. **Jeff Dye**, Audit Director, regularly taught Introductory Auditor Course modules.

Joel Grover, Deputy Assistant Inspector General for Financial Management and Information Technology Audits, serves as co-chair of the Federal Audit Executive Council's Financial Statements Committee which develops and coordinates the council's positions on a variety of accounting and auditing issues related to federal financial reporting. The committee also jointly sponsored with the Government Accountability Office an annual federal financial statement audit update conference held on March 30, 2011. Additionally, Mr. Grover serves as a co-chair of the Maryland Association of Certified Public Accountants Members in Government Committee.

Treasury Office of Inspector General Intranet Site-TIGnet

The Treasury Office of Inspector General Intranet Site (TIGnet), developed by OIG's Office of Management to provide a central location to efficiently and effectively disseminate information to all staff within the OIG, was launched on February 1, 2011. TIGnet is based upon a Windows SharePoint 2007 platform and serves as the official intranet site for all the components within OIG. The TIGnet site content will be maintained by the respective components and constantly updated with internal announcements and notifications. Our office has begun establishing document libraries, shared calendars, resource centers, and a technical helpdesk ticketing system. These new options have greatly improved the synergy within our office by making information centrally located and easily accessible to all OIG staff members. Moving forward, the ultimate goal of TIGnet is to create a completely web-based platform that will further encourage collaboration and improve efficiency within our organization using a commercial off-the-shelf platform.

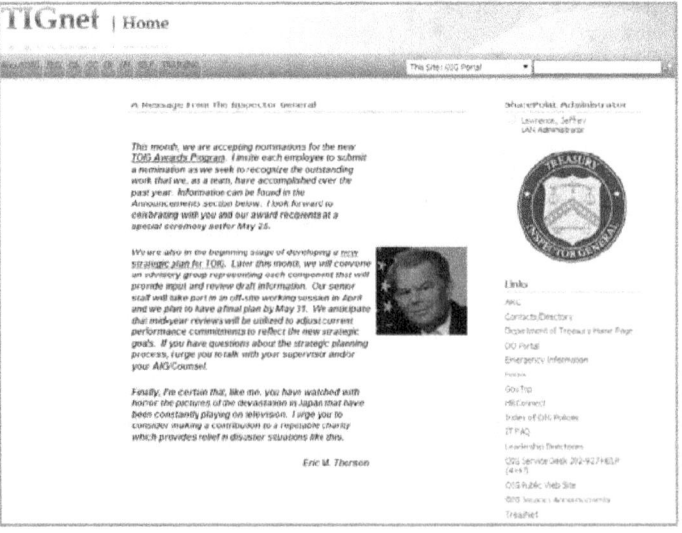

Pictured above is our TIGnet home page.

Statistical Summary

Summary of OIG Activity

For the 6 months ended March 31, 2011

OIG Activity	Number or Dollar Value
Office of Counsel Activity	
Regulation and legislation reviews	0
Instances where information was refused	0
Office of Audit Activities	
Reports issued and other products	65
Disputed audit recommendations	0
Significant revised management decisions	0
Management decision in which the IG disagrees	0
Monetary benefits (audit)	
Questioned costs	0
Funds put to better use	$ 19,607,790
Revenue enhancements	0
Total monetary benefits	$19,607,790
Office of Investigations Activities	
Criminal and judicial actions (including joint investigations)	
Cases referred for prosecution and/or litigation	28
Cases accepted for prosecution and/or litigation	13
Arrests	9
Indictments/informations	2
Convictions (by trial and plea)	8

Significant Unimplemented Recommendations

For reports issued prior to April 1, 2010

The following list of OIG audit reports with unimplemented recommendations is based on information in Treasury's automated audit recommendation tracking system, which is maintained by Treasury management officials.

Number	Date	Report Title and Recommendation Summary
OIG-06-030	05/06	*Terrorist Financing/Money Laundering: FinCEN Has Taken Steps to Better Analyze Bank Secrecy Act Data but Challenges Remain* FinCEN should enhance the current FinCEN database system or acquire a new system. An improved system should provide for complete and accurate information on the case type, status, resources, and time expended in performing the analysis. This system should also have the proper security controls to maintain integrity of the data. (1 recommendation)
OIG-08-035	06/08	*Network Security at the Office of the Comptroller of the Currency Needs Improvement* OCC should ensure that the principle of least privilege is enforced and applied to all OCC computer users as required by OCC policy. (1 recommendation)
OIG-09-024	1/09	*General Management: Treasury Should Reactivate State-Held Federal Unclaimed Assets Recovery Program (Corrective Action Verification on OIG-02-105)* Treasury should reactivate the state-held federal unclaimed assets recovery program with appropriate policies, procedures, and controls. This recommendation has a potential revenue enhancement monetary benefit of $10.5 million. (1 recommendation) It should be noted that Treasury management reported this recommendation as implemented in April 2011.
OIG-09-027	1/09	*Management Letter for Fiscal Year 2008 Audit of the Office of the Comptroller of the Currency's Financial Statements* OCC should continue to dedicate resources to fully implement the necessary System Management Server process automatically and promptly detect and remove unauthorized personal and public domain software from OCC systems (workstations) and implement controls to restrict users from downloading and installing unapproved software. (1 recommendation)

OIG-CA-09-011 07/09 *Information Technology: FY 2009 Evaluation of Treasury's FISMA Implementation for Its Intelligence Program*
Due to the sensitive nature of the finding and recommendation, we designated the report Limited Official Use. One recommendation in this report has not been implemented. (1 recommendation)

OIG-10-001 10/09 *Safety and Soundness: Material Loss Review of TeamBank, National Association*
OCC should emphasize to examiners the need to: (1) adequately assess the responsibilities of a controlling official (chief executive officer/president, for example) managing the bank to ensure that the official's duties are commensurate with the risk profile and growth strategy of the institution; (2) review incentive compensation and bonus plans for executives and loan officers; and (3) ensure that banks conduct transactional and portfolio stress testing when appropriate. (1 recommendation)

OIG-10-014 12/09 *Management Letter for Fiscal Year 2009 Audit of the United States Mint's Financial Statements*
The Mint should comply with their standard operating procedures by properly reviewing the undelivered orders report and deobligating orders that meet the criteria stated in the standard operating procedures. (1 recommendation)

OIG-10-017 12/09 *Safety and Soundness: Material Loss Review of Omni National Bank*
OCC should implement a policy for examiner in charge rotation for midsize and community banks. (1 recommendation)

OIG-10-025 12/09 *Management Letter for Fiscal Year 2009 Audit of the Office of the Comptroller of the Currency's Financial Statements*
OCC management should continue with its plan to implement a software solution to restrict users from installing and executing unauthorized software on OCC workstations. (1 recommendation)

OIG-10-035 2/10 *Management Letter for Fiscal Year 2009 Audit of the Department of the Treasury Financial Statements*
The Chief Information Officer, with input from the Office of the Deputy Chief Financial Officer, should implement the use of Secure Sockets Layer

for the Treasury Department's Information Executive Repository and CFO Vision applications. (1 recommendation)

Summary of Instances Where Information Was Refused

October 1, 2010, through March 31, 2011

There were no such instances during this semiannual period. We reported in our prior semiannual report that OIG was being denied unrestricted and unfettered access to information from OCC for use in investigations of possible fraud upon OCC by individuals of failed OCC-regulated financial institutions. Those requests for information were made pursuant to OIG's obligation to investigate issues relating to Treasury's programs and operations, which include the national bank safety and soundness examinations conducted by OCC, and attempts to interfere with or defraud those examinations. During this semiannual period, we entered into a memorandum of understanding with OCC that provides for our office to have the necessary access to information and personnel during the conduct of an investigation or inquiry involving bank fraud that falls under our jurisdiction.

Listing of Audit Products Issued

October 1, 2010, through March 31, 2011

Financial Audits and Attestation Engagement

Audit of the United States Mint's Schedule of Custodial Deep Storage Gold and Silver Reserves as of September 30, 2010 and 2009, OIG-11-004, 10/21/10

Financial Management: Report on the Bureau of the Public Debt Trust Fund Management Branch Schedules for Selected Trust Funds as of and for the Year Ended September 30, 2010, OIG-11-017, 11/5/10

Audit of Bureau of Engraving and Printing's Fiscal Years 2010 and 2009 Financial Statements, OIG-11-019, 11/12/10

Management Letter for Fiscal Year 2009 Audit of the Bureau of Engraving and Printing's Financial Statements, OIG-11-020, 11/12/10

Audit of the Federal Financing Bank's Fiscal Years 2010 and 2009 Financial Statements, OIG-10-021, 11/12/10

Management Letter for Fiscal Year 2010 Audit of the Federal Financing Bank's Financial Statements, OIG-11-022, 11/12/10

Audit of the Community Development Financial Institutions Fund's Fiscal Years 2010 and 2009 Financial Statements, OIG-11-024, 11/15/10

Management Letter for Fiscal Year 2010 Audit of the Community Development Financial Institutions Fund's Financial Statements, OIG-11-025, 11/15/10

Audit of the Department of Treasury's Fiscal Years 2010 and 2009 Financial Statements, OIG-11-031, 11/15/10

Audit of the Financial Management Service's Fiscal Years 2010 and 2009 Schedules of Non-Entity Government-Wide Cash, OIG-11-034, 11/17/10

Management Report for the Audit of the Financial Management Service's Fiscal Years 2010 and 2009 Schedules of Non-Entity Government-wide Cash, (Sensitive But Unclassified), OIG-11-035, 11/17/10

Audit of the Financial Management Service's Fiscal Years 2010 and 2009 Schedules of Non-Entity Assets, Non-Entity Costs and Custodial Revenue, OIG-11-037, 11/18/10

Management Report for the Audit of the Financial Management Service's Fiscal Years 2010 and 2009 Schedules of Non-Entity Assets, Non-Entity Costs and Custodial Revenue (Sensitive But Unclassified), OIG-11-038, 11/18/10

Audit of the Department of the Treasury's Special-Purpose Financial Statements for Fiscal Years 2010 and 2009, OIG-11-039, 11/19/10

Audit of the United States Mint's Fiscal Years 2010 and 2009 Financial Statements, OIG-11-042, 12/3/10

Management Letter for the Audit of the United States Mint's Fiscal Years 2010 and 2009 Financial Statements, OIG-11-043, 12/3/10

Audit of the Exchange Stabilization Fund's Fiscal Years 2010 and 2009 Financial Statements, OIG-11-044, 12/6/10

Audit of the Office of the Comptroller of the Currency's Fiscal Years 2010 and 2009 Financial Statements, OIG-11-045, 12/7/10

Management Letter for the Audit of the Office of the Comptroller of the Currency's Fiscal Years 2010 and 2009 Financial Statements, OIG-11-046, 12/7/10

Audit of the Department of the Treasury Forfeiture Fund's Fiscal Years 2010 and 2009 Financial Statements, OIG-11-048, 12/8/10

Audit of the Financial Crimes Enforcement Network's Fiscal Years 2010 and 2009 Financial Statements, OIG-11-049, 12/15/10

Audit of the Office of D.C. Pensions' Fiscal Years 2010 and 2009 Financial Statements, OIG-11-050, 12/15/10

Audit of the Alcohol and Tobacco Tax & Trade Bureau's Fiscal Years 2010 Financial Statements and 2009 Balance Sheet, OIG-11-051, 12/17/10

Audit of the Office of Thrift Supervision's Fiscal Years 2010 and 2009 Financial Statements, OIG-11-052, 12/17/10

Management Letter for the Audit of the Office of Thrift Supervision's Fiscal Years 2010 and 2009 Financial Statements, OIG-11-053, 12/17/10

Management Letter for Audit of the Department of the Treasury's Fiscal Years 2010 and 2009 Financial Statements, OIG-11-061, 2/24/11

Information Technology Audits and Evaluations

Fiscal Year 2010 Audit of Treasury's Federal Information Security Management Act Implementation for Its Collateral National Security Systems, OIG-11-005, 10/21/10

Information Technology: The Department of Treasury Federal Information Security Management Act Fiscal Year 2010 Audit, OIG-11-023, 11/12/10

Information Technology: Treasury is Generally in Compliance With Executive Order 13103, OIG-11-036, 11/17/10

Performance Audits – Reviews of Failed Banks Pursuant to Section 987 of the Dodd-Frank Act

Safety and Soundness: Failed Bank Review of MainStreet Savings Bank, FSB, OIG-11-001, 10/13/10 (closed July 16, 2010; estimated loss to the DIF - $11.4 million)

Safety and Soundness: Failed Bank Review of First Federal Bank of North Florida, OIG-11-002, 10/15/10 (closed April 16, 2010; estimated loss to the DIF - $6 million)

Safety and Soundness: Failed Bank Review of Home Federal Savings Bank, OIG-11-003, 10/18/10 (closed November 6, 2009; estimated loss to the DIF - $5.4 million)

Safety and Soundness: Failed Bank Review of Key West Bank, OIG-11-006, 10/25/10 (closed March 26, 2010; estimated loss to the DIF - $23.1 million)

Safety and Soundness: Failed Bank Review of Independent National Bank, OIG-11-007, 11/2/10 (closed on August 20, 2010; estimated loss to the DIF - $23.2 million)

Safety and Soundness: Failed Bank Review of First National Bank, Savannah, Georgia, OIG-11-008, 11/2/10 (closed on June 25, 2010; estimated loss the DIF - $68.9 million)

Safety and Soundness: Failed Bank Review of First National Bank, Rosedale, Mississippi, OIG-11-009, 11/3/10 (closed June 4, 2010; estimated loss to the DIF -$12.6 million)

Safety and Soundness: Failed Bank Review of Beach First National Bank, OIG-11-010, 11/3/10 (closed April 9, 2010; estimated loss to the DIF - $130.3 million)

Safety and Soundness: Failed Bank Review of Community National Bank of Bartow, OIG-11-011, 11/3/10 (closed August 20, 2010; estimated loss to the DIF $10.3 million)

Safety and Soundness: Failed Bank Review of Williamsburg First National Bank, OIG-11-012, 11/3/10 (closed July 23, 2010; estimated loss to the DIF - $8.8 million)

Safety and Soundness: Failed Bank Review of Southern Colorado National Bank, OIG-11-013, 11/4/10 (closed October 2, 2009; estimated loss to the DIF - $6.6 million)

Safety and Soundness: Failed Bank Review of Marshall Bank, National Association, OIG-11-014, 11/5/10 (closed January 29, 2010; estimated loss to the DIF - $4.1 million)

Safety and Soundness: Failed Bank Review of Bay National Bank, OIG-11-015, 11/5/10 (closed July 9, 2010; estimated loss to the DIF - $17.4 million)

Safety and Soundness: Failed Bank Review of American National Bank, OIG-11-016, 11/5/10 (closed March 19, 2010; estimated loss to the DIF - $17.1 million)

Safety and Soundness: Failed Bank Review of Valley Capital Bank, N.A., OIG-11-018, 11/8/10 (closed December 11, 2009; estimated loss to the DIF - $7.4 million)

Safety and Soundness: Failed Bank Review of Woodlands Bank, OIG-11-027, 11/15/10 (closed July 16, 2010; estimated loss to the Deposit Insurance Fund (DIF) - $115 million)

Safety and Soundness: Failed Bank Review of Imperial Savings and Loan Association, OIG-11-028, 11/15/10 (closed August 20, 2010; estimated loss to the DIF - $3.5 million)

Safety and Soundness: Failed Bank Review of First National Bank of the South, OIG-11-029, 11/16/10 (closed July 16, 2010; estimated loss to the DIF - $74.9 million)

Safety and Soundness: Failed Bank Review of Home National Bank, OIG-11-030, 11/16/10 (closed July 9, 2010; estimated loss to the DIF - $78.7 million)

Safety and Soundness: Failed Bank Review of Los Padres Bank, OIG-11-032, 11/16/10 (closed August 20, 2010; estimated loss to the DIF - $8.7 million)

Safety and Soundness: Failed Bank Review of The La Coste National Bank, OIG-11-033, 11/16/10 (closed February 19, 2010; estimated loss to the DIF -$3.7 million)

Safety and Soundness: Failed Bank Review of Maritime Savings Bank, OIG-11-040, 11/30/10 (closed September 17, 2010; estimated loss to the DIF - $83.6 million)

Safety and Soundness: Failed Bank Review of Granite Community Bank, N.A., OIG-11-041, 12/2/10 (closed May 28, 2010; estimated loss to the DIF - $17.3 million)

Safety and Soundness: Failed Bank Review of BC National Banks, OIG-11-047, 12/8/10 (closed April 30, 2010; estimated loss to the DIF - $11.4 million)

Safety and Soundness: Failed Bank Review of Security Savings Bank, FSB, OIG-11-054, 12/22/10 (closed October 15, 2010; estimated loss to the DIF - $82.2 million)

Safety and Soundness: Failed Bank Review of Ideal Federal Savings Bank, OIG-11-055, 12/29/10 (closed July 9, 2010; estimated loss to the DIF - $2.1 million)

Safety and Soundness: Failed Bank Review of First Arizona Savings, FSB, OIG-11-056, 1/3/11 (closed October 22, 2010; estimated loss to the DIF - $32.3 million)

Safety and Soundness: Failed Bank Review of First Suburban National Bank, OIG-11-058, 2/24/11 (closed October 22, 2010; estimated loss to the DIF - $30.9 million)

Safety and Soundness: Failed Bank Review of Community National Bank, OIG-11-059, 2/24/11 (closed December 17, 2010; estimated loss to the DIF - $3.7 million)

Safety and Soundness: Failed Bank Review of United Americas Bank, National Association, OIG-11-060, 2/24/11 (closed December 17, 2010; estimated loss to the DIF - $75.8 million)

Safety and Soundness: Failed Bank Review of The Bank of Miami, N.A., OIG-11-062, 3/3/11 (closed on December 17, 2010; estimated loss to the DIF - $64 million)

Safety and Soundness: Failed Bank Review of The First National Bank of Barnesville, OIG-11-063, 3/22/11 (closed October 22, 2010; estimated loss to the DIF - $33.9 million)

Other Performance Audits

The Failed and Costly BSA Direct R&S System Development Effort Provides Important Lessons for FinCEN's BSA Modernization Program, OIG-11-057, 1/5/11

Review of the Joint Implementation Plan for the Transfer of Office of Thrift Supervision Functions, OIG-11-064, 3/28/11

Supervised Contract Audit

Contract Audit: Crane & Co.'s Price Proposal in Response to Solicitation No. BEP-10-0001, OIG-11-026, 11/15/10, **$19,607,790 S**

Other Product

Joint Response by the Inspectors General of the Department of the Treasury and Board of Governors of the Federal Reserve System to a Congressional Request for Information Related to the Consumer Financial Protection Bureau, OIG-CA-11-004, 1/4/11

Audit Reports Issued With Questioned Costs

October 1, 2010, through March 31, 2011

At the beginning of the period, there were no audit reports from prior periods pending a management decision on questioned costs. There were also no audit reports issued during this period with questioned costs.

Audit Reports Issued With Recommendations That Funds Be Put to Better Use

October 1, 2010, through March 31, 2011

Category	Total No. of Reports	Total	Savings	Revenue Enhancement
For which no management decision had been made by beginning of reporting period	0	0	0	0
Which were issued during the reporting period	1	$19,607,790	$19,607,790	0
Subtotals	1	$19,607,790	$19,607,790	0
For which a management decision was made during the reporting period	0	0	0	0
Dollar value of recommendations agreed to by management	0	0	0	0
Dollar value based on proposed management action	0	0	0	0
Dollar value based on proposed legislative action	0	0	0	0
Dollar value of recommendations not agreed to by management	0	0	0	0
For which no management decision was made by the end of the reporting period	1	$19,607,790	$19,607,790	0
For which no management decision was made within 6 months of issuance	0	0	0	0

A recommendation that funds be put to better use denotes funds could be used more efficiently if management took actions to implement and complete the recommendation including: (1) reduction in outlays, (2) de-obligations of funds from programs or operations, (3) costs not incurred by implementing recommended improvements related to operations, (4) avoidance of unnecessary expenditures noted in pre-award review of contract agreements, (5) any other savings which are specifically identified, or (6) enhancements to revenues of the federal government..

Previously Issued Audit Reports Pending Management Decisions (Over 6 Months)

There are no previously issued audit reports pending management decisions for the reporting period.

Significant Revised Management Decisions

October 1, 2010, through March 31, 2011

There were no significant revised management decisions during the period.

Significant Disagreed Management Decisions

October 1, 2010, through March 31, 2011

There were no management decisions this period with which the IG was in disagreement.

Peer Reviews

October 1, 2010, through March 31, 2011

Office of Audit

Audit organizations that perform audits and attestation engagements of federal government programs and operations are required by *Government Auditing Standards* to undergo an external peer review every 3 years. The objective of an external peer review is to determine whether, during the period under review, the audit organization's system of quality control was suitably designed and whether the audit organization was complying with its quality control system in order to provide the audit organization with reasonable assurance that it was conforming to applicable professional standards.

No external peer reviews were conducted of the Treasury OIG Office of Audit during this semiannual period. The date of the last external peer review of the Treasury OIG was November 19, 2009, and was conducted by the Department of State OIG. Treasury OIG received a peer review rating of pass. There are no outstanding recommendations from this external peer review. A copy of the Department of State OIG's external peer review report is available on our website at www.treasury.gov/about/organizational-structure/ig/Documents/Treasury%20OIG%20Peer%20Review%20Final%202009.pdf.

No external peer reviews of another federal audit organization were conducted by our office during this semiannual reporting period. There are no outstanding recommendations from the previous peer review conducted by our office. That peer review was conducted on the National Aeronautics and Space Administration OIG's audit organization and was completed June 30, 2010.

Office of Investigations

The CIGIE has mandated that the investigative law enforcement operations of all Offices of Inspector General (OIG) undergo peer reviews every 3 years in order to ensure compliance both with (1) CIGIE's investigations quality standards and with (2) the relevant guidelines established by the Office of the Attorney General for the United States. In March 2011, the Small Business Administration's OIG conducted a peer review of our office and found our office to be in compliance with all relevant guidelines. There are no unaddressed recommendations outstanding from this review.

In January 2011, Treasury OIG conducted a peer review of the OIG for the Department of the Interior. Our review found the Department of the Interior's Office of Investigations to be in compliance with all relevant guidelines. There are no unaddressed recommendations outstanding from our January 2011 review.

Bank Failures and Nonmaterial Loss Reviews

We conducted reviews of 11 failed banks with losses to the DIF that did not meet the definition of a material loss in the Federal Deposit Insurance Act. These reviews were performed to fulfill the requirements found in Section 987 of the Dodd-Frank Act. As redefined in the Dodd-Frank Act, the term "material" loss which, in turn, triggers a material loss review to be performed is, for 2010 and 2011, a loss to the DIF that exceeds $200 million; for 2012 and 2013, a loss to the DIF that exceeds $150 million; and, for 2014 going forward, a loss to the DIF that exceeds $50 million (with provisions to increase that trigger to a loss that exceeds $75 million under certain circumstances).

For losses that are not material, Section 987 requires that each 6-month period, the Office of Inspector General of the federal banking agency to (1) identify the estimated losses that have been incurred by the DIF during that 6-month period and (2) determine the grounds identified by the failed institution's regulator for appointing the FDIC as receiver, and whether any unusual circumstances exist that might warrant an in-depth review of the loss. For each 6-month period, we are also required to prepare a report to the failed institutions' regulator and the Congress that identifies (1) any loss that warrants an in-depth review, together with the reasons why such a review is warranted and when the review will be completed; and (2) any losses where we determine no in-depth review is warranted, together with an explanation of how we came to that determination. The table below fulfills this reporting requirement to the Congress for the 6-month period ended March 31, 2011. We issue separate audit reports on each review to the responsible Treasury regulator, OCC or OTS.

Bank Failures and Nonmaterial Loss Reviews

Bank Name/Location	Date Closed/Loss to the Deposit Insurance Fund	OIG Summary of Regulator's Grounds for Receivership	In-Depth Review Determination	Reason/ Anticipated Completion Date of the In-Depth Review
Regulator – Office of the Comptroller of the Currency				
The First National Bank of Barnesville Barnesville, Georgia	October 22, 2010 $33.9 million	• Dissipation of assets or earnings due to unsafe and unsound practices • Unsafe and unsound condition	No	No unusual circumstances noted. However, our review revealed certain questionable transactions that were referred by our auditors to the OIG Office of Investigation.
First Suburban National Bank Maywood, Ilinois	October 22, 2010 $30.9 million	• Dissipation of assets or earnings due to unsafe and unsound practices • Unsafe and unsound condition	No	No unusual circumstances noted
The Bank of Miami, N.A. Coral Gables, Florida	December 17, 2010 $64 million	• Dissipation of assets or earnings due to unsafe and unsound practices • Unsafe and Unsound condition	No	No unusual circumstances noted
United Americas Bank, N.A. Atlanta, Georgia	December 17, 2010 $75.8 million	• Dissipation of assets or earnings due to unsafe and unsound practices • Capital impaired	No	No unusual circumstances noted
Community National Bank Lino Lakes, Minnesota	December 17, 2010 $3.7 million	• Dissipation of assets or earnings due to unsafe and unsound practices • Unsafe and unsound condition	No	No unusual circumstances noted

Bank Name/Location	Date Closed/Loss to the Deposit Insurance Fund	OIG Summary of Regulator's Grounds for Receivership	In-Depth Review Determination	Reason/ Anticipated Completion Date of the In-Depth Review
Canyon National Bank Palm Springs, California	February 11, 2011 $10 million	• Dissipation of assets or earnings due to unsafe and unsound practices • Unsafe and unsound condition	No	No unusual circumstances noted
First National Bank of Davis Davis, Oklahoma	March 11, 2011 $26.5 million	• Assets are less than obligations to creditors • Dissipation of assets or earnings due to unsafe and unsound practices • Unsafe and unsound condition • Capital impaired • Violations of laws and regulations	Yes	Unusual circumstances identified; estimated completion date is March 2012
Regulator – Office of Thrift Supervision				
Security Savings Bank FSB Olathe, Kansas	October 15, 2010 $82.8 million	• Capital impaired • Failed to submit acceptable capital restoration plan • Board of directors consented to appointment of receiver	No	No unusual circumstances noted
First Arizona Savings Scottsdale, Arizona	October 22, 2010 $32.3 million	• Capital impaired • Failed to submit acceptable capital restoration plan • Board of directors consented to appointment of receiver	No	No unusual circumstances noted
Appalachian Community Bank McCaysville, Georgia	December 17, 2010 $26 million	• Capital impaired • Board of directors consented to appointment of receiver • Assets are less than obligations to creditors	No	No unusual circumstances noted
San Luis Trust Bank FSB San Luis Obispo, California	February 18, 2011 $96.1 million	• Capital impaired • Failed to submit acceptable capital restoration plan • Assets are less than obligations to creditors	No	No unusual circumstances noted

References to the Inspector General Act

	Requirement	Page
Section 4(a)(2)	Review of legislation and regulations	27
Section 5(a)(1)	Significant problems, abuses, and deficiencies	8-21
Section 5(a)(2)	Recommendations with respect to significant problems, abuses, and deficiencies	8-21
Section 5(a)(3)	Significant unimplemented recommendations described in previous semiannual reports	28-30
Section 5(a)(4)	Matters referred to prosecutive authorities	27
Section 5(a)(5)	Summary of instances where information was refused	30
Section 5(a)(6)	List of audit reports	30-35
Section 5(a)(7)	Summary of significant reports	8-21
Section 5(a)(8)	Audit reports with questioned costs	35
Section 5(a)(9)	Recommendations that funds be put to better use	36
Section 5(a)(10)	Summary of audit reports issued before the beginning of the reporting period for which no management decision had been made	36
Section 5(a)(11)	Significant revised management decisions made during the reporting period	36
Section 5(a)(12)	Management decisions with which the IG is in disagreement	37
Section 5(a)(13)	Instances of unresolved FFMIA noncompliance	10
Section 5(a)(14)	Results of peer reviews conducted of Treasury OIG by another OIG	37-38
Section 5(a)(15)	List of outstanding recommendations from peer reviews	37-38
Section 5(a)(16)	List of peer reviews conducted by Treasury OIG, including a list of outstanding recommendations from those peer reviews	37-38
Section 5(d)	Serious or flagrant problems, abuses, or deficiencies	N/A
Section 6(b)(2)	Report to Secretary when information or assistance is unreasonably refused	30

Abbreviations

BPD	Bureau of the Public Dept
BSA	Bank Secrecy Act
CDFI	Community Development Financial Institutions
CFPB	Consumer Financial Protection Bureau
CIGFO	Council of Inspectors General for Financial Oversight
CIGIE	Council of the Inspectors General on Integrity and Efficiency
DIF	Deposit Insurance Fund
Dodd-Frank	Dodd-Frank Wall Street Reform and Consumer Protection Act
FDICIA	Federal Deposit Insurance Corporation Improvement Act
FDIC	Federal Deposit Insurance Corporation
FinCEN	Financial Crimes Enforcement Network
FISMA	Federal Information Security Management Act
FMS	Financial Management Service
FRB	Board of Governors of the Federal Reserve System
FSOC	Financial Stability Oversight Council
GAO	Government Accountability Office
IRS	Internal Revenue Service
IT	information technology
MLR	material loss review
MSB	money services businesses
OCC	Office of the Comptroller of the Currency
OCIO	Office of Chief Information Officer
OIG	Office of Inspector General
OMB	Office of Management and Budget
OTS	Office of Thrift Supervision
Recovery Act	American Recovery and Reinvestment Act of 2009
R&S	Retrieval and Sharing
SBLF	Small Business Lending Fund
SSBCI	State Small Business Credit Initiative
TARP	Troubled Asset Relief Program
TIGnet	Treasury Office of Inspector General Intranet Site
TIGTA	Treasury Inspector General for Tax Administration

Magnolias in bloom on the west side of the Treasury Building in Washington, DC